HINDUISM

Published in the United States of America by Cherry Lake Publishing
Ann Arbor, Michigan
www.cherrylakepublishing.com

Content Adviser: April C. Armstrong, Princeton University

Reading Adviser: Marla Conn MS, Ed., Literacy specialist, Read-Ability, Inc.

Photo Credits: © Shahril KHMD/Shutterstock, cover, 1; © saiko3p/Shutterstock, 5; © michaeljung/Shutterstock, 6;
© Peter Hermes Furian/Shutterstock, 8; © Work2win/Wikimedia Commons, 11; © akedesign/Shutterstock, 12;
© Sean Pavone/Shutterstock, 14; © India Picture/Shutterstock, 16; © reddees/Shutterstock, 19; © Kudryashka/
Shutterstock, 21; © Kullanart/Shutterstock, 22; © fizkes/Shutterstock, 24; © wavebreakmedia/Shutterstock, 27;
© paul prescott/Shutterstock, 28

Copyright ©2017 by Cherry Lake Publishing
All rights reserved. No part of this book may be reproduced or utilized in any form or
by any means without written permission from the publisher.

Library of Congress Cataloging-in-Publication data on file.

Cherry Lake Publishing would like to acknowledge the work of the Partnership for 21st Century Learning.
Please visit *www.p21.org* for more information.

Printed in the United States of America
Corporate Graphics

ABOUT THE AUTHOR

Katie Marsico is the author of more than 200 children's books. She lives in a suburb of Chicago,
Illinois, with her husband and children.

TABLE OF CONTENTS

CHAPTER 1

History: Roots of the Religion

Since people began recording history, they have written about the idea of a power greater than themselves. Thousands of years later, various beliefs in this power continue to shape both individual lives and entire cultures. Religion is the system people use to organize such beliefs. Religion also standardizes ceremonies and rules for worship.

Understanding Ancient Beliefs

Hinduism is the world's oldest surviving religion. Most historians think it has existed since prehistoric times! Today, Hinduism is a collection of practices belonging to several different religious groups that developed in ancient India. But it is also an entire culture based on a wide variety of customs and ideas about faith.

Shiva is one god Hindus worship.

Hindus, or people who practice Hinduism, believe in the idea of Brahman—a **divine** force present in all things. They often worship one or several gods, including Vishnu and Shiva. The many individual gods within Hinduism are said to represent this eternal, or ongoing, force.

The ultimate spiritual goal of most Hindus is for their soul—known as the atman—to be one with Brahman. They believe that, at this point, they will achieve *moksha*, or the highest level of existence. Moksha is a state of inner peace and spiritual awareness. Hindus also say it is freedom from samsara—a cycle

Hindus believe that people who do good things are given good karma.

of birth, death, and reincarnation. To them, reincarnation involves someone's atman being reborn into a new body.

According to Hindus, a person's karma, or life force, determines what kind of rebirth he or she experiences. People who are selfless and perform good works are said to have good karma. Hindus think such individuals are rewarded by being reborn into a life that brings them closer to moksha. Meanwhile, people who are evil or who lack **morality** are thought to have bad karma. They are sometimes reincarnated as animals, and it is harder for them to break the cycle of rebirth.

(For Hindus, being reborn as an animal is far less desirable than being reincarnated as a human.)

Dharma is another important feature of Hinduism. To Hindus, the power of dharma gives order to the cosmos, or universe. It is driven by everyone following certain rules and customs and fulfilling their individual responsibilities.

A Combination of Cultures

Describing the precise history of Hinduism is complicated because it doesn't trace back to one single founder. Historians say

Developing Questions

How is it possible for people to worship different gods but still practice the same religion? What other world religions involve multiple gods? Which are based on monotheism, or the belief in one true God?

The first question is a compelling question. In many cases, compelling questions don't have straightforward answers. Yet they frequently trigger interesting discussions and debates. The second and third questions are supporting questions. Supporting questions have clear-cut answers and are often used to develop responses to compelling questions.

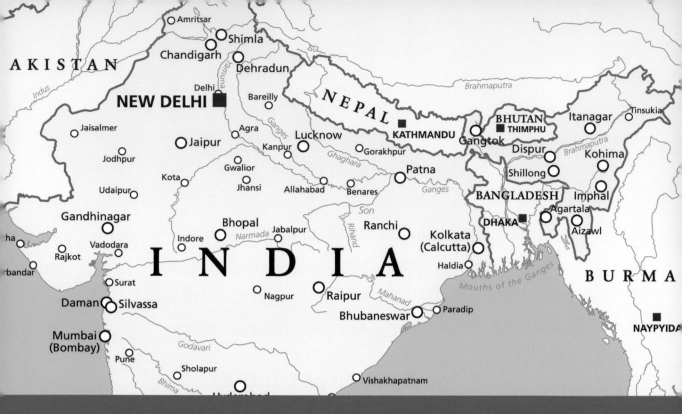

Hinduism began in northern India and what is now Pakistan.

Hinduism formed in the Indus River valley, which stretches across Pakistan and northwestern India. In about 1500 BCE, members of the Aryan culture traveled from central Asia to the Indus valley.

The Aryans introduced the Vedic religion to this area. Between 1500 BCE and 1000 BCE, they wrote the Vedas. Written in an ancient language known as Sanskrit, the Vedas were later embraced by the Hindus and so are considered to be the faith's earliest scriptures, or holy writings. They contained myths, prayers, and religious songs and poems related to samsara, karma, and dharma.

In about 700 BCE, people living in the Indus valley created the Upanishads. These scriptures are sometimes referred to as the final chapters of the Vedas. They dealt with topics such as Brahman, atman, and moksha. Much of the Vedic religion remains a mystery. Yet it seems likely that Hinduism grew as Vedic beliefs blended with those of earlier Indus valley cultures.

A Bit about the Bhagavad Gita

One of the most famous ancient Hindu texts is the Bhagavad Gita. In Sanskrit, this term means "Song of the Lord." The Bhagavad Gita is a poem that is considered part of a much larger Indian **epic**—*the Mahabharata. Historians believe the Bhagavad Gita was written between the fifth and second centuries BCE. They are unsure of its author. The main characters are a prince named Arjuna and his chariot driver, who is a form of the god Vishnu. In the Bhagavad Gita, these characters discuss the best way to achieve a spiritually meaningful life.*

CHAPTER 2

Geography: Mapping How Faith Formed

Between 500 BCE and 500 CE, the idea of bhakti began to influence the growth of Hinduism in the Indus valley. Bhakti is the belief that devotion, or displays of religious loyalty, helps people achieve the goals of their faith. It inspired Hindus to create elaborate temples, or houses of worship, across the Indian subcontinent.

Up until the sixth century, a series of emperors ruled over this entire area. In about 550, however, most of India was divided into several smaller kingdoms. As a result, separate forms of Hinduism started to take shape. They included some of the same basic beliefs. Yet individual kingdoms often focused on different gods such as Vishnu and Shiva.

This temple in Deogarh, India was built around 475 CE.

Hinduism eventually spread to other parts of Southeast Asia, such as Indonesia.

Outside Influences

As time passed, merchants and traders helped spread Hinduism throughout Southeast Asia. Meanwhile, outside cultures affected the religion's development in India. From the 15th century on, Muslim and European forces controlled much of the Indian subcontinent. (Muslims are members of the **Islamic** faith.)

Sometimes Islamic and European influences blended into the ideas and **rituals** that make up Hinduism. In turn, Hindu beliefs reached portions of Asia, Africa, and Europe that then formed Islamic and European empires. In certain cases, however, Hindus struggled to continue practicing their faith. They experienced persecution, or poor treatment, and outside pressure to **convert** to Islam or Christianity.

During the 19th century, Hinduism became a stronger feature of Indian nationalism, or national pride. Meanwhile, tensions

Gathering and Evaluating Sources

The Vedas and Upanishads are not the only examples of Hindu scriptures. The Mahabharata and the Ramayana are two others. Both are Hindu epics written between the fifth century BCE and the fifth century CE. The storyline of the Mahabharata focuses on a war between two royal families. Meanwhile, the Ramayana mainly involves the god Rama (a form of Vishnu). The plot follows his efforts to rescue his wife from a demon king. Both the Mahabharata and the Ramayana feature themes of spiritual knowledge, devotion, dharma, and good versus evil. How are these sources different from reference books? How do they both provide valuable information about Hinduism?

This temple in Atlanta, Georgia was built in 1990.

between Muslim and Hindu populations were common. In 1947, Great Britain divided India into two separate nations—India and Pakistan. Many Muslims began relocating within Pakistani borders. Hindus, on the other hand, often left Pakistan to live in the newly formed nation of India. In the late 1940s, both India and Pakistan gained independence from British rule.

The decades that followed were frequently filled with unrest. The development of new governments and disagreements over Indian–Pakistani borders led to ongoing religious persecution. Some Hindus responded by moving to Europe and North

America. After relocating in the West, they built temples and helped educate people about their faith.

Present World Populations

Today, about 1 billion men, women, and children practice Hinduism. They form roughly 15 percent of the world's population. More than 99 percent of Hindus live in Asian nations located on or near the Indian Ocean. Approximately

Promoting Peace and Tolerance

Mohandas "Mahatma" Gandhi (1869–1948) was a leader to both Indian nationalists and Hindus. At a time when the British still controlled India, Gandhi worked to achieve his people's independence. He tried to accomplish this goal through peaceful problem solving. Gandhi was also determined to unite Hindus and Muslims and to promote tolerance, or acceptance, of all religions. Ultimately, however, not everyone agreed with his message or approach, and a gunman shot him in 1948. Even though Gandhi died, many people still embrace his ideas today.

People practice Hinduism all over the world.

94 percent are found in India. Roughly 2 percent are in Nepal, and another 1 percent are in Bangladesh.

The remaining 3 percent of Hindus are scattered across the globe. About 2.3 million are in North America. The next largest Hindu populations are in the Middle East, North Africa, sub-Saharan Africa, and Europe.

Civics: Organization and Ideas

Hindus are united by shared beliefs in Brahman, atman, karma, dharma, samsara, and moksha. Yet many also support the idea that there are several different pathways to spiritual truth. This explains why there are such a wide variety of Hindu **sects**. The four major branches of Hinduism are Vaishnavism, Shaivism, Shaktism, and Smartism.

Vaishnavism

In Vaishnavism, Hindus believe Vishnu is the supreme god. They think that, every so often, Vishnu takes physical forms called *avataras*. Two of his most famous avataras are Krishna and Rama. In art, Vishnu is shown having four arms and blue skin.

Vaishnavites, or members of Vaishnavism, describe Vishnu as

Vishnu is one of the main gods in Hinduism. His job is to protect the universe.

wise, **majestic**, independent, and extremely strong. Yet they also see Vishnu as a personal being. They think that, through devotion, it's possible to develop a loving relationship with him.

Shaivism

Members of Shaivism worship Shiva as their main or only god. They believe he is a passionate, powerful being who occasionally destroys the universe. Shaivites, or followers of Shaivism, say this paves the way for the creation of a more perfect world. Artists frequently portray Shiva with a blue face and throat and a cobra necklace. According to Shaivites, Shiva also has a third eye that is a symbol, or sign, of wisdom.

Shaktism

In Shaktism, people worship the Hindu goddess Shakti. They say Shakti takes many forms and names, including Devi, Uma, Parvati, Ambika, Kali, Durga, Shitala, and Lakshmi. Sometimes she is shown holding flowers and appears to be sensitive and compassionate. In other art, Shakti is far fiercer. Certain images of this Hindu goddess feature her riding a tiger, devouring demons, or wearing a necklace of skulls. To many Shaktas, or followers of Shaktism, Shakti represents great power and strength. It's not

Developing Claims and Using Evidence

*Why do religious **icons** play such an important role in Hinduism? How do they help Hindus worship? Start by rereading the descriptions of the Hindu gods and goddesses mentioned in chapter three. Think about how each has unique features and what these features possibly symbolize. Use your ideas to develop a claim that answers the questions above. Next, find facts to back up your claim. The library, Internet, and local Hindu temples are all good places to start! (Hint: Be careful when doing online research. Web sites operated by government agencies and colleges and universities are generally reliable. Yet not all Internet sources contain accurate, up-to-date information!)*

The goddess Shakti is strong and fierce.

The god Ganesh has the head of an elephant.

unusual for Shaktas to perform a variety of rituals in the hopes of summoning **mystical** forces.

Smartism

Smartas, or Hindus who practice Smartism, worship five main gods and goddesses. Three are forms of Vishnu, Shiva, and Shakti. The other two are Ganesh and Surya. Hindus believe Ganesh is an elephant-headed god who removes obstacles, or challenges, from his followers' paths. Surya, who is known as the sun god, is shown having three eyes and four arms. He often appears in a chariot

Celebrating Faith

In Hinduism, several holidays and festivals serve as opportunities for people to celebrate their beliefs. Some of the main Hindu holy days are described below:

Holiday	When It's Celebrated	Main Theme
Holi	Late February and/or March	Two-day festival celebrating spring, color, merrymaking, and various events from Hindu mythology
Krishna Janmashtami	August and/or September	Two-day festival celebrating the birth of the god Krishna (Vishnu)
Ganesh Chaturthi	August and/or September	11-day festival celebrating the birth of the god Ganesh
Navaratri	Early October	Nine-day festival celebrating devotion to the goddess Durga (Shakti), as well as the triumph of good over evil
Diwali	October and/or November	Five-day festival celebrating the victory of light over darkness
Note: Dates often vary, depending on the geographic location of individual faith communities and the practices within different denominations.		

Some Hindus practice yoga as a form of worship.

drawn by seven horses. In Smartism, Surya is viewed as a divine healer who brings people good **fortune**.

How Hindus Worship

Hindus have many unique ways of expressing their faith. Hindu **clergy** includes priests, **monks**, and spiritual teachers called gurus. Specific religious practices depend on the beliefs of individual sects. Worship takes place in both temples and homes and usually occurs in front of a religious icon. Several Hindus make offerings of **incense**, water, flowers, and fruit to the gods.

Hindus also recite mantras, which are sounds, words, or phrases said once or many times during prayer and meditation. The process of meditation is a mental exercise involving quiet thought and reflection. Hindus meditate and perform rituals such as **yoga** to achieve inner peace and greater spiritual awareness.

Sometimes people who practice Hinduism go on pilgrimages, or religious journeys to holy sites. They often travel to rivers, where they participate in ritual bathing. Pilgrims say that entering the water washes away their sins and helps them regain purity.

CHAPTER 4

Economics: Funding a Faith

Like most major world religions, Hinduism depends on a certain amount of financial support. Examples of everyday costs include the construction and care of temples. Money is also needed to pay Hindu clergy and provide them with food and housing.

The survival of Hindu faith communities affects far more than people's opportunities to worship. Hindus view *dana*, or giving, as a key part of dharma. Temples are often involved in charity work that feeds the hungry, helps the homeless, or assists the elderly.

Means of Earning Money

Within Hinduism, donations are an important source of funding. Some Hindus commit to regular giving and offer

Some Hindus teach classes at their local temples.

10 percent of their earnings to their temple or favorite charity. Others simply donate whatever they're able to. In certain cases, Hindus make arrangements to support their religion even after their death. They set aside money for houses of worship and charitable organizations in wills and trusts. Many Hindus also volunteer their time and skills to help their temple and faith community. They teach religious education and participate in important charity work.

The rituals Hindus perform have been around for thousands of years.

Communicating Conclusions

Consider the idea of dana. Even if it is known by different names in different faiths, does the concept of dana shape other religions? To answer this question, explore charity work that local religious communities perform. How do they help others?

If you want, create a list that includes the names of nearby faith organizations and houses of worship. Write down which religion each represents, as well as the type of charity work it's involved in. Share what you learn with your family and friends. If you practice an organized religion, also discuss your conclusions with your own faith community!

[21ST CENTURY SKILLS LIBRARY]

Likely to Live On

A remarkable blend of beliefs has allowed Hinduism to survive from prehistoric times to the 21st century. Today, Hinduism represents a collection of both incredible religious ideas and cultural treasures. It is rooted in a rich past and a faith-filled present. As a result, Hinduism is likely to remain a powerful presence for centuries to come.

Taking Informed Action

Like members of all major world religions, Hindus have struggled with misunderstanding and persecution. Much of the time, a lack of knowledge is to blame for these problems. The best way to overcome intolerance is to keep an open mind—and to keep learning! Continue educating yourself about Hinduism. With your parents' help, reach out to priests, monks, gurus, or other Hindu leaders. E-mail or perhaps even set up in-person interviews to discuss any questions you have about Hinduism. As you investigate, find unique ways to share what you learn. For example, consider celebrating a Hindu holiday with your family. Or maybe discuss artwork that shows what people believe Hindu gods and goddesses look like. The more you find out, the more action you'll be able to take to end religious intolerance!

Think About It

You have read that 1 billion Hindus represent about 15 percent of the world's population. Researchers estimate that by 2050, Hinduism will have an additional 352 million followers. Yet, at that point, Hindus would make up less than 15 percent of the world's population. Based on this information, what are you able to determine about the world's population between now and 2050? Do researchers believe it will grow faster, slower, or at the same speed as the Hindu population? By 2050, do you think Hinduism will experience more or less growth than other major world religions? Why?

For More Information

FURTHER READING

Blake, Philip. *My Religion and Me: We Are Hindus*. London: Hachette Children's Books, 2015.

Glossop, Jennifer, and John Mantha (illustrator). *The Kids Book of World Religions*. Toronto: Kids Can Press, Ltd., 2013.

WEB SITES

Hindu Kids World
www.hindukidsworld.org/index.php/en/
Check out this Web site to find out more about Hindu gods and goddesses, faith stories, and rituals.

United Religions Initiative—Kids: Hinduism
www.uri.org/kids/world_hind.htm
Visit this page for more information on Hindu beliefs, holy spaces, and celebrations.

GLOSSARY

clergy (KLUR-jee) a group of people trained to lead religious groups, such as priests, ministers, and rabbis

convert (kuhn-VERT) change one's religious beliefs

divine (dih-VINE) having to do with God

epic (EP-ik) a long story, poem, or movie about heroic adventures and great battles that happened in the past or in some imaginary place

fortune (FOR-chuhn) luck or fate

icons (EYE-kahns) pictures, drawings, or other visual representations of holy figures or gods

incense (IN-sens) a substance that is burned to produce a certain smell, often as an offering to a god

Islamic (iz-LAHM-ik) of or having to do with Islam, the religion based on the teachings of Muhammed

majestic (muh-JES-tik) having the appearance or qualities of a powerful ruler

monks (MUHNGKS) men who live apart from society in a religious community according to strict rules

morality (muh-RAL-ih-tee) principles about what is right and wrong that guide your actions

mystical (MIS-tih-kihl) having a spiritual meaning that is difficult to see or understand

rituals (RICH-oo-uhlz) acts that are always performed in the same way, usually as part of a religious or social ceremony

sects (SEKTS) groups whose members share the same beliefs and practices or follow the same leaders

yoga (YOH-guh) a system of exercises and meditation that helps people control their minds and bodies and become physically fit

INDEX